Epic Cars

Acura NSX

MEGAN COOLEY PETERSON

BLACK RABBIT BOOKS

Bolt is published by Black Rabbit Books
P.O. Box 227, Mankato, Minnesota, 56002.
www.blackrabbitbooks.com

Jen Besel, editor; Grant Gould, designer;
Omay Ayres, photo researcher

Library of Congress Cataloging-in-Publication Data
Names: Peterson, Megan Cooley, author.
Title: Acura NSX / by Megan Cooley Peterson.
Description: Mankato, Minnesota : Black Rabbit Books, 2021. | Series: Bolt. Epic cars | Includes bibliographical references and index. | Audience: Ages 8-12. | Audience: Grades 4-6. | Summary: "Experience what it's like to be behind the wheel of an Acura NSX through exciting text, vibrant photography, and labeled images and other graphics"— Provided by publisher.
Identifiers: LCCN 2019027453 (print) | LCCN 2019027454 (ebook) | ISBN 9781623102524 (hardcover) | ISBN 9781644663486 (paperback) | ISBN 9781623103460 (ebook)
Subjects: LCSH: Acura NSX automobile—Juvenile literature.
Classification: LCC TL215.A256 P48 2021 (print) | LCC TL215.A256 (ebook) | DDC 629.222/2—dc23
LC record available at https://lccn.loc.gov/2019027453
LC ebook record available at https://lccn.loc.gov/2019027454

Image Credits

Alamy: DeAngelo Lee, 26 (tl); hondanews.com: Acura NSX GT3, 15 (b); Honda Acura, 3, 4–5, 6–7, 8–9 (b), 11, 15 (t), 18–19, 21, 22–23, 24, 26 (tr), 27, 28–29, 32; nsx.acura.com: 17; Acura, Cover (car), 1, 10, 16, 31; nsxhq.com: NSX HQ, 12–13; Shutterstock: Elenamiv, Cover (bkgd); Garik-Prost, 19; topspeed.com: Top Speed, 8–9 (t)

Every effort has been made to contact copyright holders for material reproduced in this book. Any omissions will be rectified in subsequent printings if notice is given to the publisher.

Contents

CHAPTER 1

Racing Down the Road

An Acura NSX zips down the road. The engine growls. The car's pointed front end looks mean and powerful. The NSX leaves most other cars in its dust.

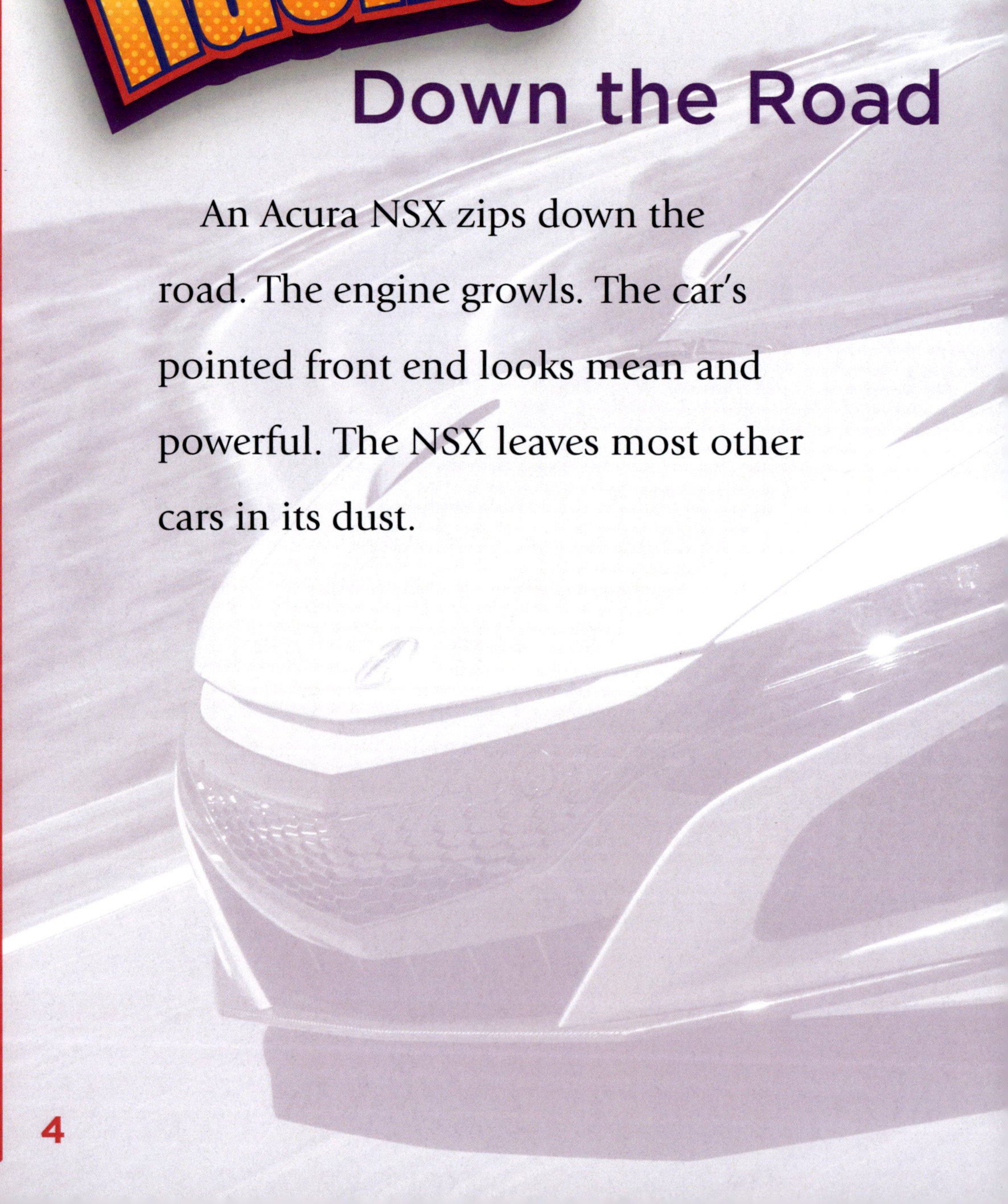

Acura released the first NSX in 1990. The company made them until 2005. It brought a new version back in 2016.

Bringing It Back

The new NSX raced onto the roads in 2016. This supercar can hit 60 miles (97 kilometers) per hour in 2.7 seconds. Its top speed is 191 miles (307 km) per hour.

1990 NSX VS. 2019 NSX

2019 NSX

TOP SPEED
191
MILES
(307 km) per hour

573
horsepower

2.7
SECONDS

TIME TO GO FROM
0 to 60 MILES
(97 KM) PER HOUR

1990 NSX

TOP SPEED
167
MILES
(269 km) per hour

270
horsepower

5.7
SECONDS

TIME TO GO FROM
0 to 60 MILES
(97 KM) PER HOUR

CHAPTER 2

Design

The Acura NSX was designed for speed. It is shaped to reduce **drag**. Air flows easily over **flush** door handles. Large air vents at the back cool the engine. Vents in the hood create **downforce**.

The NSX went through thousands of hours of **aerodynamic** testing.

PARTS OF AN ACURA NSX

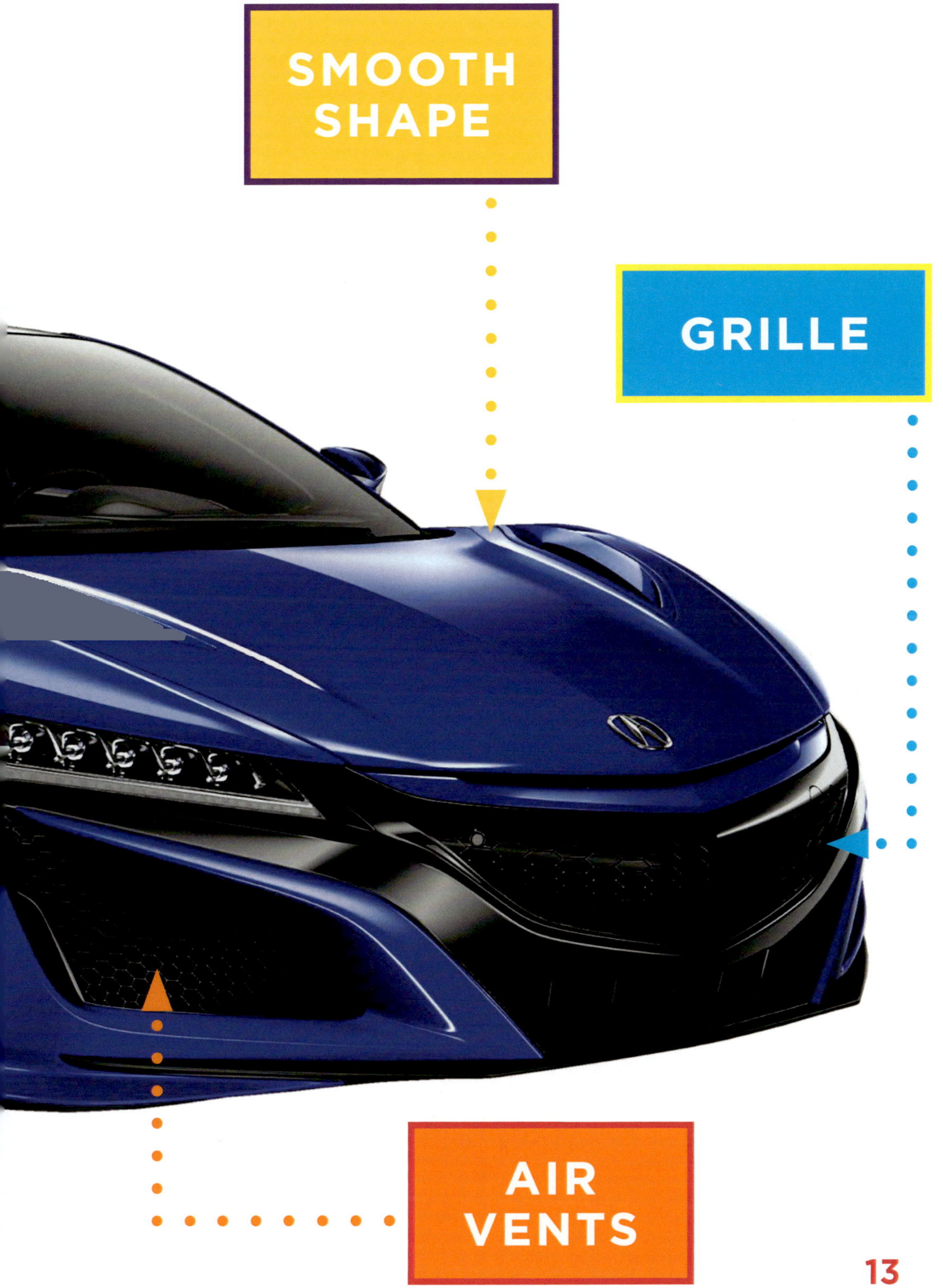
SMOOTH SHAPE
GRILLE
AIR VENTS

The Interior

The NSX's interior gives owners a race car experience. The seat hugs the driver. The steering wheel has a flat top and bottom. This shape doesn't block the driver's view of the road. It also gives drivers more legroom.

Acura made a racing version of the NSX. It's called the NSX GT3.

ACURA
AutoNation
MOTUL
AutoNation
MICHELIN

SURROUNDED BY SOUND

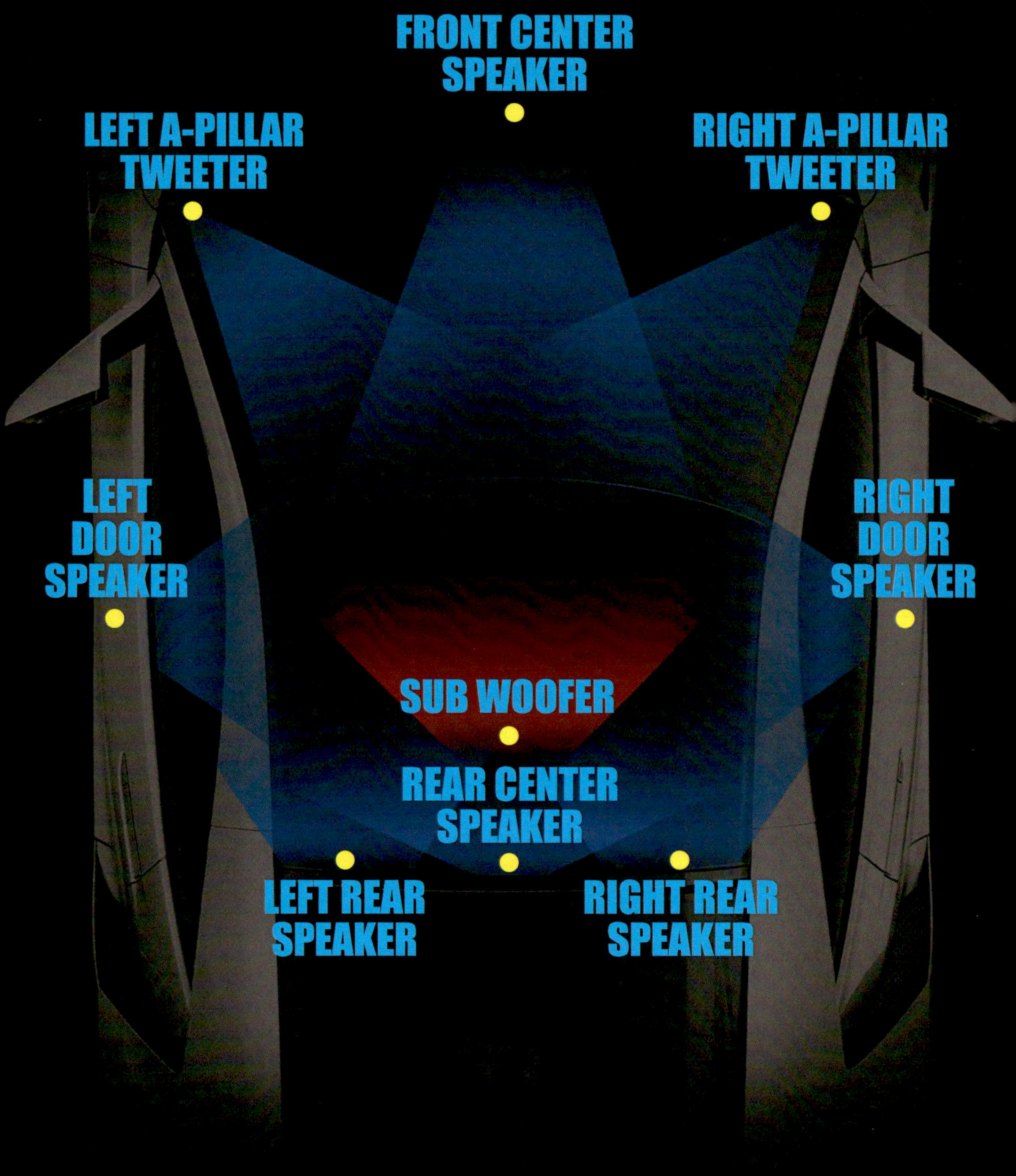

Maps and Music

The NSX comes loaded with high-tech gadgets. A touch screen displays maps and controls music. Buttons on the steering wheel also control the music. Surround sound brings music to life with nine speakers.

Personalized

The NSX makes sure drivers stand out on the street. It takes more than 20 hours to paint each NSX. Buyers can choose from eight exterior colors. Interior surfaces come in five colors. The seats also come in several color options.

Drivers can choose more than their cars' colors. The cars have four drive modes. They change how the cars handle.

DRIVING MODES

QUIET
car is quiet while driving

SPORT
best for everyday driving

SPORT PLUS
tightens steering

TRACK
makes car handle like a race car

CHAPTER 3

Power and Performance

Many supercars have an eight-cylinder engine. But not the Acura NSX. The NSX's smaller six-cylinder engine uses less gas. It also weighs less. The NSX delivers gas **mileage** of about 21 miles (34 km) per gallon.

2019 Aston Martin DBS Superleggera

2019 Acura NSX

2019 Maserati GranTurismo

2019 Bugatti Chiron

weight in pounds

TOTAL CAR WEIGHTS

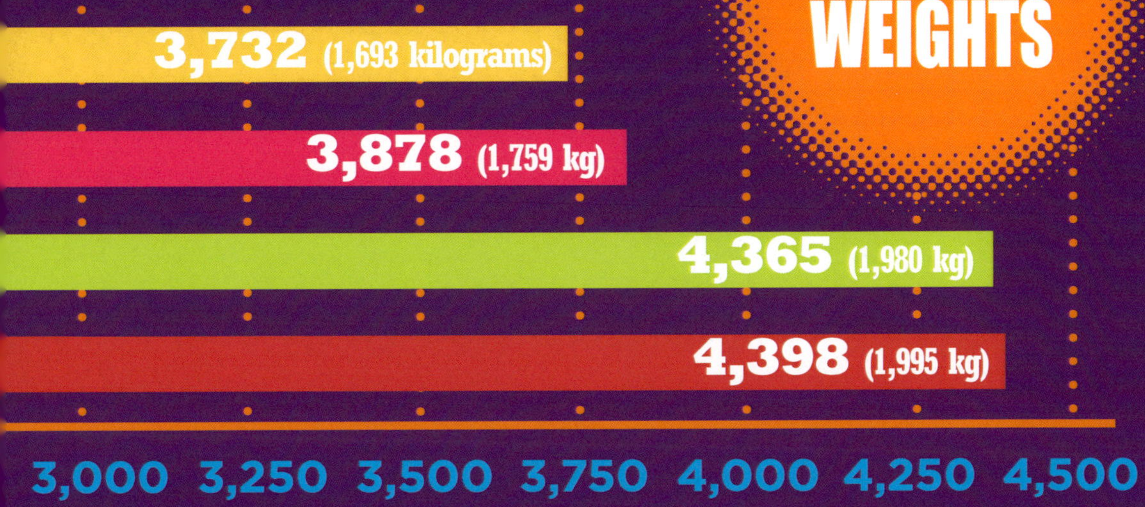

Plenty of Power

The NSX does have a smaller engine. But at 573 **horsepower**, it has plenty of muscle. The engine also has twin turbos. The turbos force more air into the engine. More air makes the engine go faster.

Each NSX engine takes five to six hours to build.

Electric Power

The NSX has three electric motors. These motors give the car extra power at takeoff. Then the gas engine takes over. The motors also help the car take sharp corners at high speeds.

By the Numbers

2

TOTAL SEATING

$159,300

BASE PRICE

47.8

INCHES

(121 CENTIMETERS)

HEIGHT

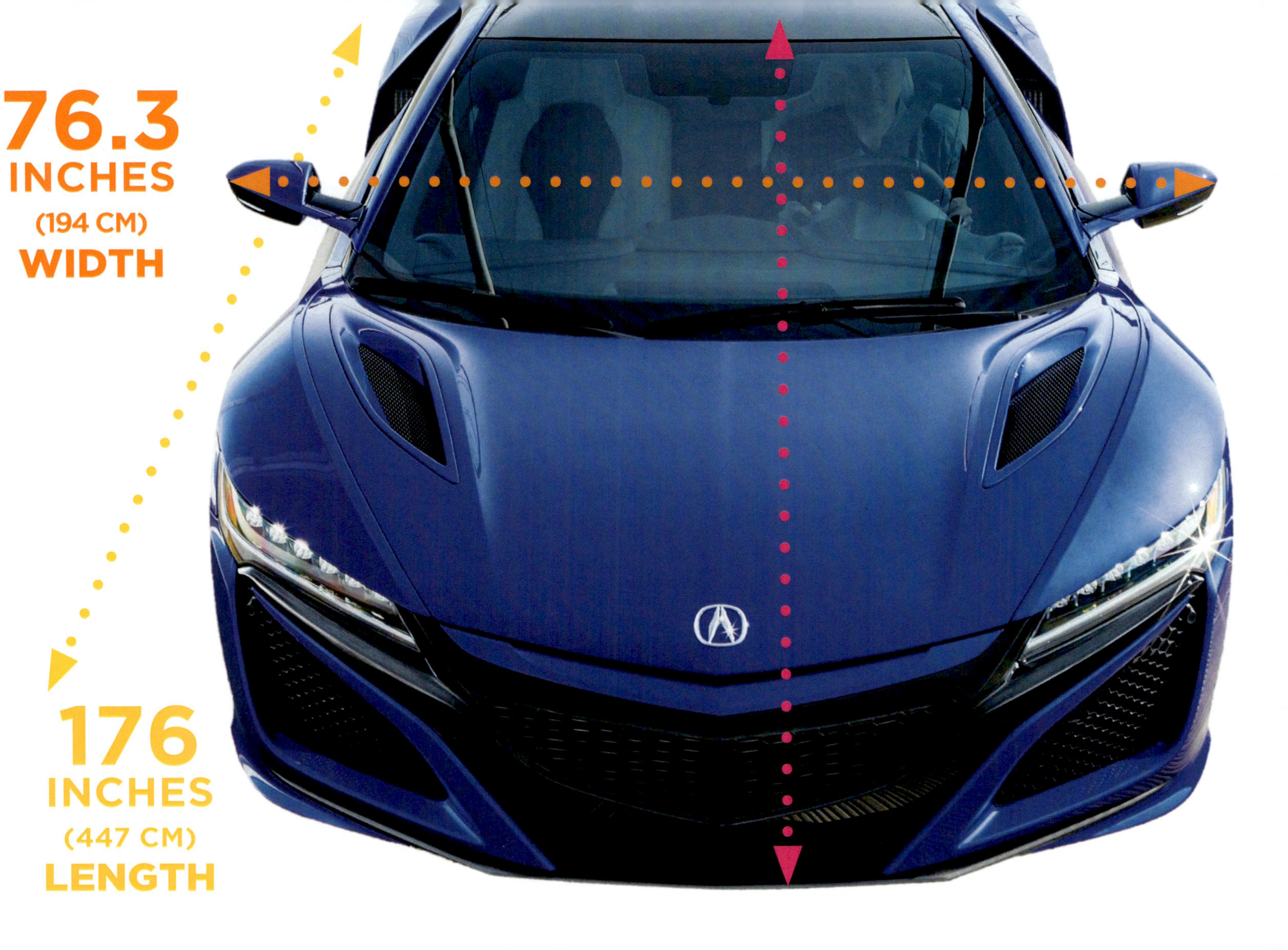

76.3
INCHES
(194 CM)
WIDTH
176
INCHES
(447 CM)
LENGTH

The NSX is one of the few supercars built in the United States.

CHAPTER 4

An Epic Car

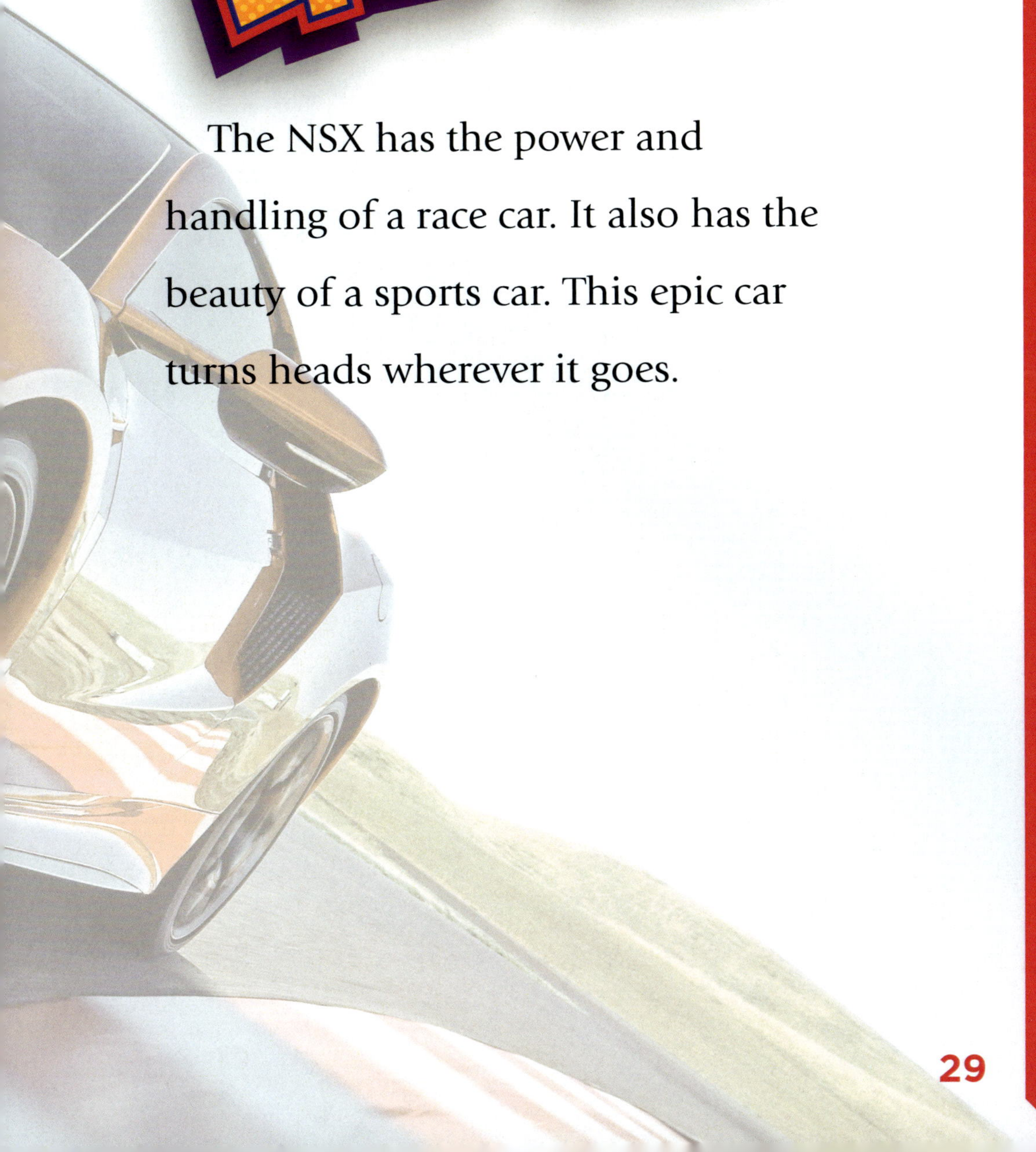

The NSX has the power and handling of a race car. It also has the beauty of a sports car. This epic car turns heads wherever it goes.

aerodynamic (air-oh-dahy-NAM-ik)—something that is shaped so it moves easily through air

downforce (doun-FAWRS)—a force that increases the stability of a motor vehicle by pressing it downward

drag (DRAYG)—something that makes action or progress slower or more difficult

flush (FLUSH)—set so it is even with the surfaces around it

horsepower (HORS-pow-uhr)—a unit used to measure the power of engines

mileage (MAHY-lij)—the average number of miles a vehicle will travel on a gallon of gasoline

release (re-LEES)—to make available to the public

spoiler (SPOI-ler)—a device placed on a vehicle to reduce lift and increase drag; it "spoils" the airflow.

LEARN MORE

BOOKS

Bodensteiner, Peter. *Supercars*. Gearhead Garage. Mankato, MN: Black Rabbit Books, 2017.

Fishman, Jon M. *Cool Sports Cars*. Awesome Rides. Minneapolis: Lerner Publications, 2019.

Niver, Heather Moore. *21st Century Cars*. Feats of 21st Century Engineering. New York: Enslow Publishing, 2019.

WEBSITES

2020 Acura NSX
nsx.acura.com

2020 Acura NSX Build & Price
nsx.acura.com/build

2020 Acura NSX Review, Pricing, and Specs
www.caranddriver.com/acura/nsx

INDEX